The Night Watch

The Night Watch

Poems by

Barbara Krasner

© 2025 Barbara Krasner. All rights reserved.
This material may not be reproduced in any form, published,
reprinted, recorded, performed, broadcast,
rewritten or redistributed without
the explicit permission of Barbara Krasner.
All such actions are strictly prohibited by law.

Cover design by Shay Culligan
Cover image: *The Night Watch* by
Rembrandt van Rijn, Public Domain
Author photo by Picture People,
Bridgewater, New Jersey (defunct)

ISBN: 978-1-63980-802-1

Kelsay Books
502 South 1040 East, A-119
American Fork, Utah 84003
Kelsaybooks.com

The paintings that inspired my poetry share a characteristic: I have viewed them personally.

Thank you to: the Rijksmuseum in Amsterdam; the Royal Museums of Fine Arts of Belgium in Brussels; Musée d'Orsay in Paris; and the Museum of Modern Art, the Metropolitan Museum of Art, the Frick Collection, the Neue Galerie, and the Guggenheim Museum in New York City.

Some of these paintings were on loan to the museum from elsewhere for special exhibits.

Each made an impression on me based on its narrative, its technique, its use of color, light, and shadow.

—Barbara Krasner

Acknowledgments

Many thanks to the editors of publications in which the following poems first appeared, sometimes in different forms:

The Ekphrastic Review: "The Appropriation of Brueghel," "Gertude's of South Orange"

The Mackinaw: A Journal of Prose Poetry: "Blades of Memory Grass"

MacQueen's Quinterly: "Dollar Princess on the Palazzo"

Main Street Rag: "Taxidermy"

Mantis: "Final *Pas de Deux* Between Daughter and Mother"

I also thank my poetry mentors Kristina Marie Darling and Matthew Lippman for their feedback and encouragement. I'm grateful for the kind words of editor and teacher Lorette Luzajic and the community she and fellow editors of *The Ekphrastic Review* have offered. One of the community members is Alarie Tennille, another Kelsay Books poet, who graciously provided a blurb for *The Night Watch,* my first ekphrastic collection.

Contents

Metamorphosis

I. Song for Amsterdam

The Louvre May Have Da Vinci's *Mona Lisa,* But the Rijksmuseum Has Rembrandt's *The Night Watch*	17
My Father Smoked the Seventeenth Century	18
Song for Amsterdam	20
The Threatened Swan	21
Modern Day Portraiture	23
An Offering in the Balance	24
Holding a Letter Is Receiving the World	25
The Appropriation of Brueghel	26

II. Fin de Siècle

When Secrecy Was the Grout Holding Shards in Place	31
Taxidermy	32
The Grooming of the Garden	33
Tidal Pool Haibun	34
The Impressionists, a Footnote Inventory	35
Monet and Renoir at the Duck Pond, Argenteuil, 1873	36
Final *Pas de Deux* Between Daughter and Mother	37
Gertrude's of South Orange	38
Yet Another Reading	39
Deep Pockets	40
The Tree of Life	41
Fin de Siècle	42

III. Be Careful What You Ask For

Strange Harvest	45
When Russian Tunics Were the Rage Before World War I	46
Dollar Princess on the Palazzo	47
The Older and Younger	48
The Red-Haired Patroness	49
Be Careful What You Ask For	50
The Same Dress Is Never Actually the Same Dress	51
Twenty-three Skidoo	52
Fiddler as Witness	53
Blades of Memory Grass	54
Inquiry	55

Metamorphosis

The artist drafts his story with pencil, his narrative stored in mind's eye, transferred and perhaps modified on paper or canvas. He picks up his palette, chooses an array of colors, selects his brush for the thickness and stroke, evaluates light and shadow. He keeps his palette knife ready to apply and smooth thick movements. The story comes to life.

I. Song for Amsterdam

The Louvre May Have Da Vinci's *Mona Lisa,* But the Rijksmuseum Has Rembrandt's *The Night Watch*

After *The Night Watch* by Rembrandt van Rijn
(the Netherlands), 1642

Let the light of the captain's hand
illuminate the sentinel path!
Let our little girl mascot with long claws

of dead chicken lend motivation
against exile threats lurking between
monument buildings, between canals.

Who protects Amsterdam in the spring of 1940?
A young girl writes in her diary
with dim lamplight, no daylight allowed.

The resistance will protect the city, the country.
Bicycles, messages, guns—all weapons
against foreign occupation.

Protect Amsterdam! Remove Rembrandt's painting,
roll it away for safekeeping until
the "All Clear" has sounded.

The Netherlanders will survive!
Like Anne Frank, the sentinels illuminate
hope and the good in people.

My Father Smoked the Seventeenth Century

After *The Syndics* by Rembrandt van Rijn
(the Netherlands), 1662

Dutch Masters invite me
to open the cigar box lid. The five men
collared in conformity ensure
that all the cigars once held
within offered consistent, reliable experience.
These officials assessed quality,
after all, grading cloth like smooth,
aged tobacco leaf wrappers.

My father smoked the cigars
that once filled the box. The
aroma lingers like Limburger.
I find a box in a drawer, open
it like a profiteer finding bounty:
His parents' citizenship papers,
a Waterman pen, a gold ring
with the Hebrew inscription,
"Pesia," the name of the grandmother
he never met. Like the syndics
of the Drapers Guild, I assess
the materials. I pack the citizenship
papers in an archival acetate sleeve.
I slip on this poor-quality engagement ring
bought from a traveling vendor
in the long-ago Polish, Austrian,
Austro-Hungarian shtetl.

My father wrapped his treasures
in the seventeenth century—
his stamp collecting paraphernalia—
glassine envelopes, tongs, pocket stock books—
or souvenirs from our road trips—
matchbooks and those cone-shaped
photo viewers that could double
as key chains.

I lost the ring and if the drapers
knew that, I would not meet
their standards of duty
and accountability.
They would never have allowed
me into their world.

Song for Amsterdam

After Self-Portrait with a Straw Hat by Vincent van Gogh (the Netherlands), ca. 1887

                Pilgrim-buckled Dutch masters,
before their images veered from canvas to cigars,
hummed hymns along merchant canals
to the Amstel River.

                Their dancing rowhouses,
swayed to the beat of the canal, hoist beams
hovering above the windows like a regiment of sentinels.

                Vermeer, van Rijn, van Gogh,
palettes of blue paint the town like today's houseboats
carried away in bicycle baskets.

                The police beagle sniffs
at strapped luggage and duty-free Gouda,
unaware of the shadows Vincent wove into his straw hat.

The Threatened Swan

> After *The Threatened Swan* by Jan Asselijn
> (the Netherlands), 1650

No longer gliding along the canal,
the swan spreads her wings
in protective robe.

Just as I do when the police
bang nonstop at two am on my front door,
twist my fifteen-year-old son's

arms behind his back, bundle
him in the back seat of their cruiser
to the local station. I follow

and my wings flare when
the police ignore reading
his Miranda rights. Even a teen

has rights. They want to roughhouse
him. I want to sleep before going
off to work in just a few hours.

He has the right to remain silent,
but that's the last thing on his mind.
He shoots off his beak.

What's a mother to do
when her smug cygnet
skitters into another's home,

drunk on spilled ale,
squawks at the fun of it all?
They release him and he refuses

to ride home with me. He wants to walk.
I am too weary to argue.
I can't think about my own comfort.

But as swan-mother, I can grow nasty,
contort my body, aim my wingtips
like slender firearms at threats

or cup my swan-child in my feathers
for one more day, then send him outward
bound for his own survival.

Modern Day Portraiture

*After Frans Snyders by Anthony van Dyke
(the Netherlands), ca. 1620*

There in the West Gallery, Frans Snyders's
face was my Dutch boss staring back at me.
The shape of the face. The discerning look
that said, *I don't believe you when you say that.*
The judgmental hands. The conformity
of business attire that reflected how he wanted
all his employees to act the same way.

But I'm not an extrovert. I don't have
a ready laugh. I'm not an engineer.
I understand you inherited me. But
then you placed me under someone
the same level as me, even someone
with the same first name, so that I had
to change mine so I wouldn't completely
    disappear.

I heard you returned to the Netherlands.
I hope you learned how to be more
open in America and brought that back
to the tall townhouses with narrow
twisted stairs.

An Offering in the Balance

After *Mistress and Maid* by Johannes Vermeer
(the Netherlands), ca. 1666–1667

The maid is a woman of action, hired
to do a job. *Take the letter!* There's the tile floor
to wash, the clothes to wash
and hang dry. A Dutch home
must be immaculate, she knows that.
A domestic servant must also
be efficient. The letter arrived. She brought
it directly to her mistress. *Take it!*

> *Who is this letter from?*
> The mistress contemplates the envelope
> just as she thought hard about her ermine
> and pearls, eventually coming to conclusions
> as tight as her ringlets.

Take the letter! You write letters all morning.
You're bound to receive a few. Don't
you expect responses?

> *Who is the letter from?*

Holding a Letter Is Receiving the World

After Woman Reading a Letter *by Johannes Vermeer
(the Netherlands), 1662–1663*

It used to be I chose stationery, curled
my vowels, angled my consonants then.
Holding a letter is receiving the world.

I'd come home, find envelopes, cancelled stamps, hurled
sentences from my friends, time and again,
stories on the page, their narrative pearls.

The ink has dried bearing no one's cursive swirls.
It's all now, now, now and when, when, when.
Holding a letter was receiving the world.

Boxed stacks of rubber-banded letters squirreled,
a ruled reminder of bygone days spent,
stories on the page, their narrative pearls.

Nothing in my mailbox, nothing to unfurl.
Only emails, texts, slide-right messages sent.
Holding a letter was receiving the world.

The Appropriation of Brueghel

After *Massacre of the Innocent* by Pieter Brueghel the Elder (Flanders), 1566

I.
Hapsburg armor storms the Flemish village in search of young boys to satisfy the order to kill. Double-headed eagles scour in both directions. No one can escape the scrutiny. Parents plead in vain.

II.
The routine was always the same. Prof. C strode into class just a minute before start-time, arms full of loose papers. She insisted someone open a window for fresh air, no matter the weather. She taught medieval German literature and Norse mythology. In the days before classroom computers, she introduced our small class of German majors to the art of Pieter Brueghel the Elder. She presented him as a German painter.

III.
Bringing Spanish rule over the Dutch, say Brueghel's bristles, is no different from the *Massacre of the Innocents*. The Spanish have hired German mercenaries.

IV.
In Brussels, I rush to the Brueghel exhibit in the Royal Museums of Fine Arts of Belgium, Musée Old Masters Museum. I cannot leave Brussels without paying homage to Brueghel. "*I found him*," I want to shout to Prof. C, long since deceased. Brueghel's style pulses community portrait.

V.
Prof. C claimed this Flemish painter for Germany well before Germany occupied Belgium in the spring of 1940. Despite a birth record registered in Croyden, England in the summer of 1933, despite her appearance as a British immigrant on the SS *Veendam* to New York in 1952, presumably to begin attending the college where she would later teach, Prof. C had a thick German accent.

VI.
Like Brueghel, she focused on the minute, the small moments and made them seem important and vital to a larger environment. Open the window, breathe the air, become anyone you want to be.

II. Fin de Siècle

When Secrecy Was the Grout Holding Shards in Place

After View of the Saint Martin Canal by Alfred Sisley (France), 1870

When blue, black, and gray
tesserae formed watery mosaic.

When pedestrians and barges
waltzed to the beat of d'Orsay clock.

When nothing really extraordinary
happened. In public.

When a Madame Bovary lurked
behind canal townhouse doors.

Taxidermy

After *The Butterfly Hunt* by Berthe Morisot
(France), 1874

We traipse the campgrounds
with butterfly nets, wanting
and not wanting
to catch a being
so delicate, its mosaic
so magnificent, wanting
and not wanting
to pin its wings
forever in cotton and encase
in glass frame.

I surveil a monarch,
yellow, orange, black
brilliance and try to cup
it in my hands, protect
it from nets, feel
its velvet nap. I whisper,
Ça va? Its wings flutter.
It does not land.

The Grooming of the Garden

>After *Young Woman Knitting* by Berthe Morisot
>(France), 1883

Among the roses, she knits to show
off her latest couture. She could be anyone.

Her features, indistinct. It's the clothes
that matter. The grooming of the garden.

One purl at a time is how one rises
to middle class from hired nanny.

If only an eager suitor could see her,
take possession of the empty chair

and turn it toward her. Then
she could lay down her knitting needles.

Tidal Pool Haibun

After *Surf, Isle of Shoals* by Childe Hassam
(US), 1913

Memory and forgetting collide in white clusters against ancient rock, and only when the tide recedes, will know who won the war.

What we remember:
ocean waters spray toward land
if we can catch them.

The Impressionists, a Footnote Inventory

[1]Light pours into the Musée d'Orsay through the Belle Époque ironwork of this former train station. It's all about light and shadow. [2]The Renoir painting of the fields where white wildflowers glow. [3]Light shimmers at the top of Monet's water lilies and dissipates into darkness toward water's depths. That same light bifurcates the Seine in Monet's view of Giverny where he chases the merest sliver of color. Light is fleeting and takes color with it. He uses a limited palette even in showing how sunlight hides in the skirt folds of his women with parasols. [4]I consider where there's light, there must be shadow. Shadow has color, contrasting color. [5] The green of Degas's background is set against the red ballerina bodice. Never use black for shadow. The trick is to see the color, not the object. [6]This is not water. This is a series of white and variegated blue blocks. [7]This is not a field, but clusters of orchid and cornflower blue, sunrise and sherbet orange, forest and hunter green. [8]Paint how it looks until an impression forms.

        Outside only gray
  city rain holds color hostage
       my umbrella frees

Monet and Renoir at the Duck Pond, Argenteuil, 1873

After *The Duck Pond* by Claude Monet (France), 1873
and *The Duck Pond* by Pierre-Auguste Renoir (France), 1873

I see eight ducks approaching the bridge.

> I see eight white ducks and two black.
> They near the far end of the bridge.

The chimney of the house stands stark against the orange roof.

> I think it's wider than that. And there's a person approaching the pond.

No, there's not. Wait, I see three more ducks at the far end.

> More blue, more blue.

More maize, more orange.

> It's autumn. It's harvest.

>> Is this your painting or mine?

Final *Pas de Deux* Between Daughter and Mother

After *Camille on Her Deathbed* by Claude Monet
(France), 1879

Your eyes are closed, but I know you hear me.
Can you see Mama? Your arms reach for her.
You say nothing, only your moaning pleas.

Papa? You see him, wrinkle your nose. He
wanted you to change the world, make it stir.
Your eyes are closed, but I know you hear me.

Shayne Leah, I say, smooth your brow. We
tangle in a *pas de deux* death dance, purr.
You say nothing, only outstretched arms plea.

You are back in Brooklyn, on narrow streets,
playing stickball, until you learn to flirt.
Your eyes are closed, but I know you hear me.

I will help you cross. It is me you need.

Gertrude's of South Orange

After *Before the Mirror* by Édouard Manet
(France), 1876

For my wedding, my mother visited her favorite
dress shop and chose a V-necked royal blue dress
with silver metallic threads and beads
running down the bodice like Debussy
water pearls. Even without a tiara
on her perfectly coiffed auburn hair,
my father guided his queen down
the red carpet of brick stairs
to the Cadillac. Her diamond
drop necklace, diamond earrings,
and diamond watch signaled her royalty.

She held her head high, straightened
her back and shoulders until
osteoporosis and widowhood took hold
and the most valued crown jewel an inhaler.

Yet Another Reading

After *The Reading* by Édouard Manet
(France), 1869

Yet another suitor,
yet another reading
of Shakespeare's sonnets.

    "Thou art lovelier than a summer day!"
    "Two loves have I of comfort and despair!"
    "My love is as a fever burning still!"

Give her a young man
who knows how to read
a poem with feeling,

who knows which words
to accent and which to not,
when to slow down or speed up.

She relies on the painter
for relief. She appears
ready to pounce

from her padded perch
into the garden
where she can dream

and recite these sonnets
    from memory, burning.

Deep Pockets

After Rehearsal of the Ballet Onstage by Edgar Degas (France), 1874

The ballet master knows the men
are not thinking of their wallets.
He has a performance to produce,
his dancers must not be distracted.
He claps the corps to attention
and instructs them away from
waxed moustaches and drooling lips.

Three men ogle the young ballerinas
as they prance and plié. Their patrons
expect to inspect their investments
and if one of those investments
were to accompany them
to a late supper with a bribe
to the *maitre d', c'est la vie.*

The Tree of Life

After Kitchen Garden, Trees in Flower, Spring, Pontoise
by Camille Pissarro (France), 1877

Like the Nordic Yggdrasil, the ancient tree
stands in judgment of the people in the house
it screens. Evaluation is quick, harsh, a dash.
You, monsieur, must treat your wife with respect.
You, madame, must not skimp on the butter.
To demonstrate its opinion, its flowering branches
droop. This tree is what catches the eye.
It must be adored, must be seen as grander
than sky, more majestic than white stucco.

Fin de Siècle

After *The Album* by Edouard Vuillard
(France), 1894–1895

I have come to the Met with a notebook.
and a fellow writer. I want to create
an album of my responses to art.
In the Annenberg Collection
of Nineteenth and Twentieth-Century
Masters, the hues of this painting
call out to me. A collage of images
and color, a salon of Debussy and Gide
that once graced the Natanson Paris apartment,
the home of the journal *La Revue Blanche*.

I imagine myself on the velvet divan,
close my eyes to bloodred roses and
water lilies, while Debussy's water droplets
cascade in the terrace garden. My pen catches fire.

III. Be Careful What You Ask For

Strange Harvest

After *Defeated: Service for the Dead* by Vasily Vereshchagin (Russia), 1878–1879

"A field where a thousand corpses lie"
—Stephen Crane, *War Is Kind*

Do not weep young man, for war is kind.
This is the tenth war between Russia and Turkey.
Come, read from your prayer book.

>   Oh, God of spirits and all flesh,
>   give rest to the souls
>   of Thy departed servants
>   in a place of brightness, refreshment,
>   and repose.

>   Young men ran with scimitar and rage
>   toward their enemy for the glory of Russia,
>   its name still on their lips as color drains.

Do not weep, young priest, for war is kind.
The incense you wave into the field scents
and blesses the fallen martyrs of victory.

>   Picked clean of their uniforms and gold
>   teeth, their mouths still agape in surprise,
>   they rest in their shrouds of rotting flesh and allegiance.

Do not weep, dear reader, for war is kind.
We forget the power-hungry rants of years past,
the control of the Balkans that led to battle.

>   The clouds descend upon the field
>   sending memory-erasing pellets. Battle
>   can begin again, even on the same field.

When Russian Tunics Were the Rage Before World War I

After *Portrait of Werner Miller* by Ferdinand Hodler (Switzerland), 1899

Werner Miller stares at me the way my grandmother's cousin, Moishe Adler, did, tunic-clad boys who played with metal soldiers before one remained in neutral Switzerland and one escaped to it.

A tunic gave them movement, even if belted.

My great-aunt Doba wore a Russian tunic before she died in the flu pandemic of 1918. But she was born and lived in Russia.

When I met with Moishe, now Murray, in Marina del Rey, he wore a blue plaid sports coat, the tunic, like his parents and sister, rounded up in Vienna and shot upon arrival in Minsk, a tucked-away memory.

Dollar Princess on the Palazzo

After *Flaming June* by Frederic Leighton
(Great Britain), 1895

This ripe apricot wants

to rest her shoulder against soft surface,
not rigid coat and tails, not celluloid collar

and pomaded hair, not pince-nez'd.
No epaulets or medals and ribbons.

Let her hair fall loosely where it blends with blankets,
not braided and spun in the day's fashion,

body draped in exotic thoughts,
travel the world without a trunk, dive into the sea,

close her eyes to the heat on a camel in the desert,
not confined by corset and bustle.

As her oleander tonic takes root,
she enters that fine space between

temporary and final sleep, that valley
where she's worth more than her father's money.

The Older and Younger

After The Two Sisters *by James Tissot*
(France), 1863

She studied German.
        I studied German.
She entered publishing,
        I entered publishing.
She dated and married a local boy
        named Mike.
I dated a local boy
        named Mike. I did not marry him.

She drove us to the arts cinema
to see *Der Blechtrommel*. I won't
eat eel to this day. We swayed
at the Beacon Theater
to the jazz riffs of the Rippingtons,
and the stylings of Phil Perry and Najee.

"The Umbrellas of Cherbourg" played
at her wedding. Only I knew
she wanted me to be her
maid of honor, but there were
two sisters between us.

No umbrella could shield me
from the chasm our mother's death
created. My sister closed the book
on my outstretched fingers until

she started on Mounjaro.
        So did I.

The Red-Haired Patroness

After *Symphony in Flesh Color and Pink*
by James McNeil Whistler (US), 1873

Flesh tones and pink hues suit Mrs. Frances Leyland's fine complexion, her gaze into the flowering almond branches. Her gossamer gown of almond flower appliques embraces the carefully chosen rug and parquet floor. Only she would curate a dressing gown to match the decor of her London townhouse. Not one layer of her frock disappears into the nothingness of her existence. For she is Mrs. Frances Leyland, not merely Mrs. Frederick Leyland.

Be Careful What You Ask For

After *Madame X* by John Singer Sargent
(US), 1884

The gown's thin straps are so scandalous
that Madame wants to pull the portrait
from the salon. But this is not what her
portraitist first painted.

                        That right strap,

      resting in the nest
      between neck and shoulder,

once draped lazily across the upper arm.

Her skin is almost blue, maybe purple.

          The bodice a bustier   the skirt black satin.
          Her embarrassment
                      his best work.

The Same Dress Is Never Actually the Same Dress

After *Three Sisters* by Léon Frederic
(Belgium), 1896

because the manufacturer
can claim although the pattern is the same
each was cut separately
sewn separately
pressed separately
hung separately
even if brought home together
in a single Abraham & Straus bag
and paid for with a single credit card.

Twenty-three Skidoo

After *Dust Storm* by John Sloan
(US), 1906

Nearly seventy years before I worked
in the Flatiron Building, seventy years
before I followed my sister in studying German,
seventy years before I followed
my sister into publishing, dust could have pushed
me along Twenty-third Street and Fifth Avenue.

Now I understand why we never
opened the windows and even without
opening the windows, the sills filled
with soot.

Fiddler as Witness

> After *The Green Violinist* by Marc Chagall
> (Russia/France), 1923–1924

In the former Warsaw Ghetto,
a cut-out of Chagall's *Green Violinist*
rests against a park bench,
accompanied by a cut-out
of native son Isaac Bashevis Singer.

The fiddler stands on the roof
of Sholom Aleichem, a pair
of unmatched boots so
the occupiers, this time Russian,
won't want them.

My grandfather
floats above the wooden huts
of Borisov, heads west from Minsk
to America, exchanges his belted tunic
for a western suit, his carpentry
tools for the assembly line.

Blades of Memory Grass

After *Christina's World* by Andrew Wyeth
(US), 1948

I sit in the kitchen after staging's complete, the house ready for sale. The walls scream for me to hold onto them. The wall phone where my father taped photos of my mother's hands, rings in my ears. The stovetop diagrams erased by decades of Brillo call for me to ignite the burners. The textured tile floor no longer awaits bare feet and cartwheels. The staging people ripped up the navy carpeting in the dining room revealing a century-old hardwood floor. But frame shadows on tufted wallpaper suggest abandoned wedding photos except for mine, which was banished to the basement. Inside yet outside, yearning for a place I can't have. I remember the day in 1965 I wear ankle socks with new black patent leather shoes from Levy's, run down the front brick stairs to show our neighbor across the street. I trip, and my sister holds my head in her lap while the doctor stitches my knee. Another day, 1968: I lie on the front lawn after running through the sprinkler, contemplating my future as cloud shapes suggest. My body crunches the plastic-like grass and I pull at milkweed and dandelions. I find a buttercup and place it under my chin. I cannot see its reflection.

Inquiry

> After *The Woman in Gold* by Gustav Klimt
> (Austria), 1907

A German once painted
me with his eyes, wrapped my neck
with his heart in silver curlicues.

But I always returned. I wanted
but never asked for his signature
on my portrait of gold.

About the Author

Barbara Krasner is a New Jersey-based poet and historian who leaned into ekphrastic writing in early 2024 as a way to heal from a rare, incurable autoimmune disease. A Best of Microfictions and multiple Pushcart Prize nominee, her work has appeared in more than sixty literary journals, including *The Ekphrastic Review, MacQueen's Quinterly, Blaze/VOX, The Mackinaw: A Journal of Prose Poetry,* and *The Jewish Writing Project.*

She is the author of two poetry chapbooks, *Chicken Fat* (Finishing Line Press, 2017) and *Pounding Cobblestone* (Kelsay Books, 2018). Her novel in verse, *Ethel's Song: Ethel Rosenberg's Life in Poems* (Calkins Creek, 2022) co-won the Paterson Prize for Books for Young People, Grades 7–12.

Barbara holds an MFA from the Vermont College of Fine Arts and a Ph.D. in Holocaust & Genocide Studies from Gratz College, where she teaches in its graduate programs. She is also co-editor of *Kelsey Review,* literary magazine of Mercer County Community College, where she teaches in the history and English departments and serves as director of the Mercer County Holocaust, Genocide & Human Rights Education Center.

Visit her website at:
www.barbarakrasner.com

www.ingramcontent.com/pod-product-compliance
Lightning Source LLC
Chambersburg PA
CBHW030742170426
43193CB00028BA/867